THE TWENTIETH CENTURY AND
THE HARLEM RENAISSANCE
A HISTORY OF BLACK PEOPLE
IN AMERICA
1880-1930

Written by:
Stuart Kallen

THE TWENTIETH CENTURY AND THE HARLEM RENAISSANCE
A History of Black People in America 1880-1930

Published by Abdo & Daughters, 4940 Viking Dr., Suite 622,, Edina, Minnesota 55435

Library bound edition distributed by Rockbottom Books, Pentagon Tower, P.O. Box 36036, Minneapolis, Minnesota 55435

Library of Congress Number: 90-083618   ISBN: 1-56239-019-8

Cover Illustrations by: Marlene Kallen
Inside Photos by: Bettmann Archive
              The Granger Collection

Reprinted 1993 by Abdo & Daughters.

Cover Illustrations by: Marlene Kallen

Edited by: Rosemary Wallner

TABLE OF CONTENTS

Sharecropping

CHAPTER 1
THE CENTURY OF SLAVERY ENDS

The Struggle Continues

By 1890, almost eight million black people lived in the United States, most of them in the South. The majority of these blacks were rural workers whose main skills were farming and growing cotton. But years of cotton growing had worn out the soil in the South. Growing cotton was not as profitable as it had once been. Many freed black people had no money for land and supplies and were forced to work for their former owners. Many white farm owners lent black people seeds for crops and let them live on their land in one-room cabins. When the crops were harvested, the black tenants were supposed to get a share of the profits. This practice was called *sharecropping*. But dishonest bookkeeping and overcharging kept the sharecroppers broke and destitute year after year. The system was not much different than slavery.

Cotton prices reached an all-time low after a depression during the 1870's. Agricultural workers, both white and black, had a "hard row to hoe."

The Ku Klux Klan had succeeded in keeping blacks from voting by using terror, lynchings, and murder. Between 1890 and 1990, over 1,300 mob murders against blacks were reported in the South. In 1900 alone, 114 black people were hung, burned, or shot. Life was not much better in the North. Rampaging white mobs killed blacks and burned their homes and businesses on hundreds of occassions. This terror kept blacks away from voting, and in 1901, the last black United States congressman, George White, left office. The United States Congress and Senate, once again, had no voices speaking for black people. From the President on down, racial discrimination was a topic that was ignored by government officials. The pattern was the same in state and local governments.

Industry and Black People

After the Civil War, Northern money men came into the South and bought up much of its shattered economy. The South was rich in water power, iron, coal, and oil; all of the necessary ingredients for the industrial revolution. Factories and railroads were built using underpaid black labor. When the factories opened, the jobs went to white workers. If blacks were hired in the factories at all, it was for heavy labor at the lowest wage.

The skilled black workers from the Civil War days — brickmasons, printers, painters, carpenters, and mechanics — found their jobs given to white workers who refused to work with blacks. Generally, the only jobs open to blacks were road building, sewer digging, street cleaning, rock quarrying, furnace stoking, and mining. One third of all black workers were female domestic servants — laundresses, maids, house cleaners, and cooks. These were the lowest paying jobs in America. Most of the unions that were fighting for the protection of white workers refused admission to blacks. Some black workers formed their own unions.

The worst exploitation of black workers was the "convict lease system" or chain gang. If a black man committed a petty crime, like stealing food for his hungry family, he was given a long sentence on the chain gang. Once on the chain gang, the convict was dressed in black-and-white striped clothes, chained together at the ankle with other prisoners, and forced to build roads, dig ditches, and farm crops. Chain gangs were leased to private industries. The state was paid money while the convict did backbreaking labor in the hot sun for no pay. Once again, the system was not much different than slavery.

CHAPTER 2
VOICES OF HOPE

Although the early years of the twentieth century were difficult ones for most black people, there were voices of hope in the darkness. Organizations were formed by gifted black people in an effort to help the average black person rise above prejudice and discrimination. From the ashes of hatred, cries of protest rose in unison.

Here are the profiles of a few great black leaders from the early 1900's.

W. E. B. DuBois — 1868-1963
Author, Civil Rights Leader

William Edward Burghardt DuBois is considered the greatest black leader of the early twentieth century. He was a gifted scholar, writer, and advocate for human rights.

W. E. B. DuBois was born in Great Barrington, Massachusetts. His parents were of African, French, and Dutch ancestry. DuBois was a gifted student and graduated from high school at the age of fifteen. He was accepted to Fisk University in Nashville, Tennessee. During the summers, DuBois taught poor black children in dirt-floored, log cabin schools. After graduation, DuBois attended Harvard University in Massachusetts where he was the first black man to receive a Ph.D. from that institution. After leaving Harvard, DuBois wrote his first book, *The Suppression of the Slave Trade*. Soon, he became a professor of Latin, German, Greek, and English at the University of Pennsylvania. DuBois continued to teach history, economics, languages, and write books at several universities.

W. E. B. DuBois

Not contented with just teaching, DuBois became involved with several organizations that demanded equal rights for black people all over the world. Beginning in 1900, DuBois organized a series of conferences where he demanded self-government and independence for countries in Africa that were under European rule. DuBois fought for more than fifty years to free Africa of oppressive European-run governments.

In 1903, DuBois published *The Souls of Black Folks*, a book about the problems that black Americans faced in everyday life. The book soon became a best-seller. In 1905, DuBois gathered together a group of black leaders and educators at Niagara Falls, New York. The group, known as the Niagara Movement, demanded full rights for all black people. This group was the forerunner of the National Association for the Advancement of Colored People, or NAACP. The NAACP still fights for equal rights for black people in the 1990's.

Because of DuBois's support, the NAACP grew rapidly. By 1916, it had 9,000 members in sixty-seven cities. When a suspicious police agent asked DuBois just what the NAACP was demanding for blacks, DuBois replied, "the enforcement of the Constitution of the United States." DuBois continued to work with the NAACP until 1934.

DuBois was the chairman of the Department of Sociology at Atlanta University until 1944. While there, he wrote hundreds of essays and articles and several books. But DuBois was frustrated by continued racial discrimination. After World War II, DuBois became involved in socialism and the peace movement, which wanted to ban nuclear weapons. Because of these involvements, the United States government tried to put him in jail.

At the age of eighty-two, DuBois was forced to go on trial for speaking his mind. At his trial, he made this statement: "It is a sad commentary that we must enter a courtroom today to plead Not Guilty to something that cannot be a crime — advocating peace and friendship between the American people and the peoples of the world." Letters of protest against the trial poured in from all over the world. Fortunately, the judge dropped the case against Dubois.

13

Even though the government could prove no wrongdoing by DuBois, his reputation was ruined. Books and magazines that were afraid of controversy refused to publish his writings. Organizations would not hire him as a speaker. The Federal Bureau of Investigation tapped his telephone and opened his mail. He was not allowed to travel outside the country until 1958.

When he was ninety-three years old, DuBois joined the Communist Party. In 1963, he gave up his United States citizenship and moved to Ghana, Africa. He died there on August 27, 1963.

Although DuBois had many troubles with the United States government, his influence is still felt. Because of his work with the NAACP, DuBois has helped give black people a voice for over seventy-five years.

Ida B. Wells-Barnett — 1862-1931
Civil Rights Leader

Between the years 1890 and 1900, over 1,200 blacks in the United States were hung by lynch mobs. Ida Wells-Barnett compiled a record of all these bloody lynchings and called it "A Red Record." A magazine printed the Red Record, and tens-of-thousands of people became aware of the problem and tried to put a stop to it. Because of the bravery of Ida Wells-Barnett, the number of lynchings in America decreased.

Ida Wells was born a slave in Mississippi. When she was sixteen years old, both her parents died within one day of each other. Wells lied about her age to get a teaching job. Her twenty-five-dollar-a-month salary supported her and her five brothers and sisters. When she complained about the shabby conditions in the school, she was fired.

Wells began writing for *Free Speech,* a newspaper in Memphis, Tennessee. Because of her writing, subscriptions to the paper increased dramatically. Her strong stand against racism caused bigoted people to threaten her life.

Ida B. Wells-Barnett, Civil Rights Leader

In 1892, three black men were dragged from the Memphis jail and lynched. Ignoring death threats, Wells printed the names of the men who did the lynching and the names of the city officials who allowed it to happen. Wells wrote articles asking blacks not to use the Memphis streetcar line, and if possible to leave town entirely. Within months, the streetcar line was almost bankrupt and over 2,000 black people had moved away from Memphis.

During the early part of the century, lynching was considered an acceptable way to deal with black criminals. But the men whose lynching Wells wrote about were not criminals. They had been jailed on phony charges because they were successful grocery store owners who were competing with a white-owned grocery store. Wells thought that if the men in Memphis were innocent, many other men who had been lynched might also have been innocent.

Wells started traveling around the country. She interviewed people who had witnessed lynchings and investigated the circumstances that caused the lynchings. Of the 728 lynchings that she investigated, about one-third were people who had actually been accused of crimes. Most of the victims did not even get a trial. They were simply dragged from the jails by mobs, beaten, and hung in the nearest tree. Many lynch victims were murdered for "quarreling with whites" or "race prejudice." Women and children were also victims of lynch mobs.

Ida Wells continued to write angry editorials. She tried to shame police, judges, and mayors into stopping the lynchings. One of her editorials caused an angry mob to burn her newspaper office in Memphis. Wells was out of town when it happened, but afterwards she was forced to move to New York City. On June 5, 1892, the *New York Age* published an article by Wells. In it, she listed all the names, dates, places, and gory details of hundreds of lynchings. The paper sold 10,000 copies.

In 1895, Wells married a lawyer, Ferdinand Lee Barnett. Together they organized black political groups and women's organizations. Wells-Barnett was one of the founders of the NAACP. Because of her efforts, people began to look at lynching as a horrible crime. It took the efforts of Ida Wells-Barnett to change people's attitudes.

Mary Church Terrell — 1863-1954
Advocate for Women's Rights

Mary Church Terrell was the daughter of a former slave, Robert Church. Her father had become wealthy selling real estate. Church went to Oberlin College in Ohio and received her masters degree in 1888. Her father disowned her because he thought that no man would want her if she studied higher mathematics. Church pursued her education and later married Robert Terrell, a judge in Washington, D.C. In 1895, Mary Church Terrell was appointed to the Board of Education in Washington, D.C. She was the first black woman in the country to hold such a position. Unfortunately, Terrell had difficulties with people who believed that women were inferior to men. She decided to fight back.

Terrell joined the women's groups who were fighting for the passage of the Nineteenth Amendment to the Constitution. The amendment would give women the right to vote. But the white women's groups that she was involved with did not want a black woman in their group. They were afraid it would hurt their position with Southerners. (Eventually the Ninteenth Amendment was passed.)

When World War I started, many black people moved north. They wanted to work in the factories that were left shorthanded when the white workers left to join the army. Because black women did not have protection from unions, Terrell organized the Women Wage-Earners Association. The union organized black nurses, waitresses, and domestic workers. Terrell also helped organize the National Association of Colored Women and the NAACP.

Terrell never gave up the struggle for equal rights. At age ninety, she organized a boycott of Washington, D.C., department stores that refused to serve blacks. She also led a march on restaurants that refused blacks. Until the day she died, Mary Church Terrell fought for the rights of women and black people.

CHAPTER 3
BLACK INVENTORS

The era of the late nineteenth and early twentieth century was an age of inventions. Motorcars, electric lights, cameras, and other inventions changed many people's lives. Before the Civil War, slaves were not allowed to hold patents, but free black men were. While white inventors made money and gained fame with their inventions, black inventors remained relatively unknown. But blacks were responsible for many inventions that changed the world. Some of them are still in use today.

Jan Ernst Matzeliger — 1852-1889
Inventor
What Jan Matzeliger did for our feet was quite a feat. Matzeliger invented a machine that could stitch the bottoms on shoes in record time. He revolutionized the shoe industry around the world.

Jan Matzeliger was born in Dutch Guiana (present-day Suriname) in South America. His mother was a black native of Guiana and his father was a wealthy Dutch engineer. Matzeliger went to work in a machine shop when he was ten years old. When he was nineteen years old, he worked aboard a ship. When the ship docked in Philadelphia, Pennsylvania, Matzeliger decided to stay in the United States.

In 1876, Matzeliger began to work for a shoe company in Lynn, Massachusetts. But working was not enough for Matzeliger. He also went to night school to learn physics. In his spare time he gave art lessons and painted.

While working at the shoe factory, Matzeliger was troubled at the amount of time it took to stitch the bottom of a shoe to the top. Every shoe had to be stitched by hand. Workers could only make forty pairs of shoes a day. Working at his home at night, Matzeliger invented a machine that automatically stitched shoes together. His first model was made from wood, wire, and cigar boxes. Matzeliger was offered fifty dollars for the machine but rejected the offer.

Jan Ernst Matzeliger

Matzeliger's Shoe Stiching Machine.

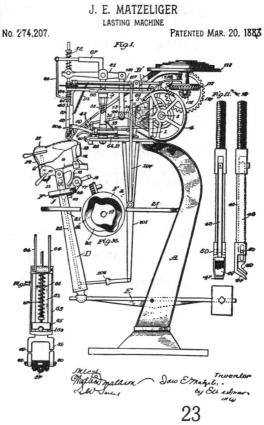

J. E. MATZELIGER
LASTING MACHINE

No. 274,207.   PATENTED MAR. 20, 1883

23

In 1880, Matzeliger invented a better version of the shoe stitching machine. This one earned him an offer of 1,500 dollars. Although he needed the money, Matzeliger turned down the offer. In 1883, Matzeliger received a patent from the U.S. Patent Office for his shoe stitching machine. The drawings of it were so complicated that a scientist from the Patent Office had to see the machine in action so that he could understand it. Matzeliger's machine enabled a worker to produce up to 700 pairs of shoes a day.

With several other men, Matzeliger started the United Shoe Company. Within a few years, they manufactured 98 percent of the shoes made in the United States. Soon the company was worth 20 million dollars.

Unfortunately, Matzeliger's money could not buy him health. In 1886 he became ill with tuberculosis. He died in 1889 and left all of his money to the North Congregational Church, the only church that had not rejected him because of his race. Sixty-five years after Matzeliger's death, the United Shoe Company was worth over one billion dollars. His technique for making shoes is used all over the world.

Lewis Howard Latimer — 1848-1928
Draftsman, Inventor

When Alexander Graham Bell invented the telephone, the plans for it were drawn up by his friend Lewis Latimer, a young black draftsman.

Latimer was born in 1848 in Boston, Massachusetts. His father deserted his family when he was ten years old, and Latimer was forced to go to work. When Latimer was eighteen years old, he worked as an office boy for a company that specialized in patenting inventions. The company employed several draftsmen (artists who specialize in drawing plans and inventions). Latimer became fascinated with drafting and bought a set of secondhand drafting tools. With the help of library books and the advice of other draftsmen, Latimer became an expert at drafting. Soon, he was the chief draftsman at the company where he had started as an office boy.

During the course of his work, Latimer met Alexander Graham Bell, and the two became good friends. Bell asked Latimer to make the drawings for the first telephone. Soon, Latimer began working on his own inventions. In 1881, Latimer started working on electricity.

He invented the Latimer Lamp, an improved light bulb that lasted longer and worked better than previous light bulbs. As a result of his invention, he was asked to help with the installation of electric light plants in New York City. He also worked with an electric company in England.

In 1884, Latimer was asked to be a member of the Edison Pioneers, a small, exclusive group of scientists who worked with Thomas Edison. Latimer continued to invent until his death in 1928.

George Washington Carver — 1864-1943
Scientist

Perhaps the most famous black scientist is George Washington Carver. It was Carver who invented one of America's favorite foods, peanut butter. In fact, Carver invented 325 products that use the peanut, including facial powder, coffee, wood stains, ink, shampoo, vinegar, and soap.

George Carver was born in 1861 on a plantation in Missouri that belonged to Moses and Susan Carver. His parents were slaves, and when he was just a baby, he and his mother were kidnapped by slave raiders and taken to Arkansas. Young George was returned to the Carver Plantation in Missouri, but his mother was never found. Carver was sick as a child and was not able to do much work. He spent most of his time wandering in the woods, collecting plants and flowers.

Carver taught himself to read, and at age ten, he left the plantation to work at odd jobs and attend school. Carver was an excellent student when he attended high school in Kansas. He won a scholarship to Highland University but the school refused him admission when they found out he was black. Carver continued to work and save money. Several years later, he was accepted at Simpson College in Iowa. He supported himself by ironing clothes for his fellow students.

At Simpson, Carver decided to become a scientist. In 1891, he enrolled in the Iowa Agricultural College where his work in botany and chemistry earned him the respect of his teachers. Carver was asked to work at the college after graduation. There, he became an instructor and the director of the greenhouse. Soon, Carver was conducting important research into funguses that were attacking wheat, oats, and soybeans. In 1896, Carver received a letter from Booker T. Washington asking him to teach at Tuskegee Institute in Alabama.

Tuskegee was an all-black college started by Washington. It did not have much lab equipment and was a poor school that could not pay Carver much of a salary. Carver did not care about the money and decided to teach at Tuskegee.

George Washington Carver, American Botanist

He said, "It has always been the one great ideal of my life to be of the greatest good to the greatest number of people."

The soil in Alabama had been worn out from years of growing cotton. At Tuskegee, Carver invented a system of crop rotation using peanuts. Peanuts were planted in cotton fields where they replenished the soil with minerals. The peanuts improved the soil. The program worked so well that soon there was an oversupply of peanuts. To solve this problem, Carver came up with many uses for peanuts. Soon, farmers were making more money farming peanuts than they were from cotton.

Besides the peanut, Carver experimented with the sweet potato. He developed 118 products that could be made from the sweet potato, including dyes and synthetic rubber. Word of Carver's inventions earned him world fame. He was visited by the crown prince of Sweden and the Prince of Wales. Henry Ford offered Carver 100,000 dollars a year to work for Ford Motor Company. Thomas Edison made a similar offer. Carver turned them both down because he wanted to teach. He said, "Education is the key to unlocking the golden door of freedom."

Carver lived out his life caring little about money or material possessions. His research is still valued by scientists today. And anybody that ever enjoyed a peanut butter and jelly sandwich owes a thanks to George Washington Carver.

Granville T. Woods — 1856-1910
Inventor

Granville T. Woods was known as the "Black Edison." In his lifetime he patented more than sixty inventions. His genius changed the transportation systems in America's cities and the way Americans communicated.

Woods was born in Columbus, Ohio, in 1856. He was forced to quit school and go to work at age ten. Woods worked as a fireman and engineer on the railroads. At age twenty-two, he studied electrical engineering on the British steamship *Ironsides*.

In 1884, Woods started a machine shop in Cincinnati, Ohio, and began manufacturing telegraph, electrical, and telephone equipment. He patented an improved telephone transmitter that was immediately bought by American Bell Telephone Company of Boston. Woods patented seven more telegraph devices by 1887, including a machine to telegraph messages to moving trains. During the next fifteen years, Woods invented air brakes for trains, steam boilers for ships, and conducting systems for trolley cars. His most important invention was the electrified "third rail" that powers subway systems. That invention made possible the modern subway systems that are in use in cities all over the world.

Although Woods sold his patents to General Electric, Westinghouse, and Bell Telephone Company, he died a poor man. When Woods accused American Engineering Company of stealing his patents, they sued him for lying. Although Woods was not lying, the legal fees used up most of his money before his death in 1910.

Granville T. Woods

World War I: Sargeants of the 369th, Black Regiment: J. H. Jones, R. Flower, C. E. Davis, J. White, J.H. Carmen, S. C. Farrell, B. Lucas, H. L. Printer, E. N. Barrington.

CHAPTER 4
BLACKS IN WORLD WAR I

The United States entered World War I in 1917. Many blacks wondered if they would be treated with equality by the country they were called on to defend. Sadly, the answer was no. When the Army started drafting men, a higher percentage of blacks were drafted than whites. Blacks were forced to serve in segregated units with inferior equipment and hostile, insulting, white commanders.

At first, blacks could not serve as officers. The Army then said that if two hundred college educated blacks signed up, they would be sent to a special officer training school. Much to the Army's surprise, 1,500 black college men signed up. Fort Des Moines in Iowa trained about 600 black officers. Blacks, however, were not allowed in the Marines and were only allowed in the Navy as menial workers.

Black servicemen were denied access to theaters, restaurants, and public transportation. Even the YMCA kept blacks out of their organizations on military bases. There were hundreds of fights and riots as a result of these and other actions. In 1917, a race riot in St. Louis resulted in the death of thirty-nine blacks. Other riots occured in Texas and South Carolina. The units involved were shipped to the worst war zones in Europe.

During the war years, like before, blacks were murdered by lynch mobs. Many people who condemed the Germans for similar murderous actions looked the other way when white violence occured against blacks in the United States. In 1919 alone, twenty-five different race riots occured in the United States. Black school principals were lynched, young boys were murdered, soldiers in uniform were burned alive.

Once black servicemen went to Europe, the discrimination continued. Most of the black troops were assigned to fight with French battalions who were locked in deadly combat with the German Army. The United States instructed the French not to treat the black soldiers as equals. But the battle-worn French Army ignored the bigoted American advice. Many black soldiers

received the distinguished Croix de Guerre
(Cross of War), France's highest military honor.

Private Melville "Doc" Miller was sixteen when he joined a group of Black American combat soldiers who became the 369th Infantry Regiment during World War I.

In spite of the discrimination, black troops fought bravely for the United States. The Germans called the all-black 369th Infantry unit "Hellfighters" because they never retreated and never were captured. Two men in the 369th, Sergeant Henry Johnson and Private Needham Roberts fought off thirty German soldiers. They killed four and wounded ten but were finally captured. Although seriously wounded, Johnson and Roberts escaped. Their bravery saved the lives of hundreds of other men in their regiment.

When World War I ended, President Woodrow Wilson said that "The world is safe for democracy." Unfortunately, for the black people in the United States, true democracy and justice still remained out of reach.

CHAPTER 5
THE HARLEM RENAISSANCE

By the end of World War I, the Harlem area of New York City had become the largest urban black community in the world. Black people from Jamaica, Haiti, Cuba, Puerto Rico, Africa, and other places mingled with American blacks from the North and South. The result was a lively mixture of cultures and languages. The crowded streets of Harlem were alive with the musical styles of jazz, rumba, ragtime, spirituals, and even string quartets. A crazy quilt of languages and accents rang out in the Harlem night. Black artists, poets, musicians, authors, and actors flocked to Harlem to take part in the vigorous revival of the arts that came to be known as the Harlem Renaissance.

In 1924, Alain Locke published *The New Negro.* The book was a collection of poems, essays, stories, and pictures that were produced by blacks. The book became very popular among white New Yorkers. Suddenly, white people were traveling to Harlem to browse at art galleries and dance at black music clubs. After the fad caught on in New York, it spread across the country. White people in other American cities began supporting the black cultural arts. Black people looked to the arts as a way of easing racial tensions.

New dance crazes invented in Harlem swept across the nation. Out of the Savoy Ballroom in Harlem came the Charleston and the Lindy Hop. Playwrights and songwriters began writing with black themes. *The Emperor Jones, Porgy and Bess, Blackbirds,* and other plays came to Broadway. Black actors were honored the world over. The musical styles that were invented by black Americans, blues and jazz, were selling millions of records. Alain Locke said that for black people, the twenties was a "spiritual coming of age." Here are some profiles of people who made America sit up and take notice during the Harlem Renaissance.

Marcus Manasseh Garvey — 1887-1940
Black Leader

Sixty years after the Civil War ended, millions of blacks were still suffering at the hands of discrimination. White, European governments had taken over almost every country in Africa. Africans were slaves to European laws and European greed in their own countries. Black people began demanding the freedom to make their own rules and live their own lives without white interference. Into this movement stepped Marcus Garvey who offered to lead the black people to the Promised Land.

Marcus Garvey was born in St. Ann's Bay, Jamaica. Because of poverty, Garvey, the youngest of eleven children, was forced to leave school and become a printer's apprentice at age fourteen. Garvey worked as a professional printer until he was twenty-two years old. That year he joined a strike. When the workers were defeated Garvey was banned from working as a printer in Jamaica. After briefly working on a banana plantation in Costa Rica, Garvey moved to England.

Marcus Garvey

Garvey worked for a publisher during the day. He attended the University of London at night. At the university, Garvey met many African students who told him about the movement to free Africa of white rule. In 1914, Garvey went back to Jamaica and organized the Universal Negro Improvement and Conservation Association and African Communities League (UNIA). The group wanted to make Africa the "defender of Negroes the world over."

Garvey decided to start a black college in Jamaica like Tuskegee Institute in Alabama. He wrote to Booker T. Washington and made plans to visit Tuskegee. By the time Garvey arrived in the United States, Washington had died. Garvey decided to tour the United States and speak to blacks about the UNIA.

Garvey was attracted to Harlem because of the many Jamaicans who lived there. In 1917, Garvey reorganized the UNIA in Harlem to try to create a powerful black nation in Africa. Garvey wanted the UNIA to organize and educate black people all over the world. Many white people who were prejudiced against blacks supported the UNIA. Even the Ku Klux Klan supported it. But Garvey took no funds from white organizations and would not let white people join his movement. Garvey toured the country giving rousing speeches. "Up, you mighty race!" Garvey shouted, "You can accomplish what you will . . . No one knows when the hour of Africa's redemption cometh . . . One day, like a storm, it will be here!"

In 1918, Garvey started the *Negro World,* a newspaper whose slogan was "Africa for the Africans." The *Negro World* soon became the most popular black newspaper in the country. Garvey established the Black Star Steamship Line to transport blacks back to Africa. He also started the Black Cross Nurses, the African Legion, the Black Eagle Flying Corps, and the Negro Factories Corporation. Members of these organizations dressed in fancy uniforms and held rallys and marches. Before two years passed, Garvey had raised ten million dollars.

In 1921, Garvey organized a month-long UNIA rally in Harlem. Bands, receptions, rallies, and parades entertained 25,000 blacks from all over the United States and twenty-five other countries. Garvey was voted the President-General of Africa. At the end of the month, thousands of other Harlemites joined the rally. A parade of 50,000 black people marched and danced down

Lenox Avenue in Harlem to the sounds of trumpets and drums. A mass meeting was held at Madison Square Garden. The Garveyites sent a message to the League of Nations that demanded "the right of Europe for the Europeans, Asia for the Asians, and Africa for the Africans . . . at this time when four hundred million Negroes demand a place in the sun . . ."

Unfortunately, Garvey's hopes soon crashed to the ground. His steamship company went bankrupt and he was arrested for mail fraud in connection with selling bad stock in his Black Star Corporation. In 1923, Garvey was tried in federal court. He was sentenced to five years in prison and fined 1,000 dollars. He appealed the verdict and lost. Garvey was sent to Alabama Penitentiary. His newspaper was termed as "dangerous to the comfort and security" of whites. In 1927, President Calvin Coolidge commuted his sentence and ordered him deported to Jamaica. He moved to London in 1935 and died there, penniless, in 1940.

His grand schemes had failed, but Garvey gave black people something to believe in. Self-respect and self-determination became a way of life for millions of black people thanks to Marcus Garvey.

Langston Hughes — 1902-1967
Poet, Author

More books were published by black authors and poets during the twenties than in any other previous decade in American history. Almost all of the authors lived in Harlem. The premier poet of the Harlem literary movement was Langston Hughes. He wrote about black experiences with a stark reality that many poets were afraid to express.

Langston Hughes was born in Joplin, Missouri, in 1902. His father left home shortly after he was born. As a result, Langston was raised by his grandmother, Mary. Mary Langston's first husband was an abolitionist who fought to end slavery. He was killed fighting alongside John Brown at his famous raid in Harpers Ferry, Virginia. All Mary had to remember her husband by was a bullet-riddled, bloodstained shawl that he had worn during the raid. When Langston was young, Mary would wrap herself in the shawl and tell him stories about Frederick Douglass, Harriet Tubman, and other famous abolitionists. When Langston slept, Mary would drape the shawl over him.

Langston began writing his own poetry at age thirteen. When he was nineteen years old one of his poems was published in *The Crisis,* the most famous black magazine in the country. The poem, entitled "The Negro Speaks of Rivers," told of the black connection with the Nile, the Congo, and the Mississippi rivers. The last line reads, "My soul has grown deep like the rivers." The poem, originally scribbled on the back of an envelope, is one of Hughes' most famous.

Hughes went to Columbia University in 1921, but his heart was in Harlem where the literary movement was gaining worldwide recognition. Hughes left college after one year and worked as a sailor on a freight ship. On board the ship, Hughes wrote dozens of poems while he traveled to Africa and Europe. He lived for a while in Paris where he spent most of his time listening to black jazz musicians in the Paris nightclubs. When he returned to the United Staes, Hughes continued to frequent jazz nightclubs.

Hughes moved to Washington, D.C., in 1924 where he worked as a busboy at the Wardman Park Hotel. Hughes showed his poems to Vachel Lindsay, a poet who was staying at the Wardman.

Lindsay read Hughes's poems to an audience and the response was overwhelming. Soon Hughes was gaining fame reading his poems to large audiences.

Hughes published a book of poetry in 1926 while enrolled at Lincoln University in Philadelphia. He wrote several books, and in 1930, published his first novel *Not Without Laughter*. It was an immediate success. For the next several years Hughes traveled around the globe and spent a year in the Soviet Union. In 1934 he published *The Ways of White Folks*. In 1937, Hughes returned to Harlem and started the Suitcase Theater where his plays packed the house night after night. Later, he founded theaters in Los Angeles and Chicago.

Over the years, Hughes wrote plays, poems, novels, children's books, histories, biographies, and radio and television scripts. His writing made him famous in his lifetime. Libraries and bookstores still carry his books today. Langston Hughes is considered required reading for anyone interested in the hope, pain, humor, and anger surrounding black people's lives in America.

Langston Hughes

William Christopher Handy — 1873-1958
Musician, Songwriter

Although W. C. Handy did not live in Harlem, his contribution to the music world paved the way for other black entertainers. Many of Harlem's best and brightest musicians were influenced by Handy. His name holds an honored place in black music history that few could match.

William Christopher Handy was born in Florence, Alabama. His mother predicted that his large ears meant he would be a musician. She was right. As a child, Handy made music with broom handles, combs, jugs, harmonicas, and just about anything else he could find. When he grew older, Handy traveled all over the country playing with small bands. Life on the road was not easy for a black man. Handy faced intolerance and discrimination everywhere he went. In many small towns, black men were not welcome after dark. Handy responded by writing, "I hate to see that evening sun go down." Handy wrote many blues classics, including "St. Louis Blues," "Memphis Blues," and "Beale Street Blues."

Willaim Christopher Handy

When Handy traveled through the South, he secretly passed out copies of the black newspaper, the *Chicago Defender*. This was a very brave thing to do. The paper urged Southern blacks to move north where there were better jobs and schools and less prejudice. Because white Southerners did not want their supply of cheap, black labor moving North, they outlawed the *Defender* and lynched anyone handing it out. Sheriffs pulled black people off trains that were traveling north. Despite the constant fear of beatings and lynchings, Handy continued to write hit songs.

In 1918, Handy established the Handy and Pace Music Company. The company became an instant success publishing jazz and blues songs. Before the twenties, blues music was considered to be the music of poor, ignorant blacks. Thanks to W. C. Handy, this attitude was changed. Although Handy went blind in 1943, he continued to write and publish the music of black Americans. Today, blues is a respected musical form, in part because of the father of the blues, W. C. Handy.

Louis Armstrong — 1900-1971
Musician

There were hundreds of "hot" musicians in Harlem in the twenties. The swinging sound of jazz music was taking the country by storm. One of the hottest musicians in Harlem was Louis "Satchmo" Armstrong, a trumpet player from New Orleans.

Louis Armstrong was born in 1900 on the Fourth of July. His family was very poor, and he was sent to live with his grandmother when he was five years old. Armstrong grew up in a section of New Orleans that was famous for its musicians and bands. When he was nine years old, he sang on street corners for pennies.

On New Year's Eve 1913, Armstrong was arrested for shooting off a pistol at midnight. A judge sent Louie to the Colored Waif's Home for Boys. At the home, Armstrong learned to play the cornet. When he was released, he began playing jazz in local bands. To earn enough money to live, Armstrong also washed dishes, hauled coal, and collected junk. Louis played so well that Joe "King" Oliver, a nationally famous musician, helped him perfect his playing.

Louis Armstrong

55

By the time he was eighteen years old, Armstrong was playing music full time. After playing for a year on a Mississippi riverboat, Armstrong moved to Chicago where King Oliver's band was playing. Armstrong's incredible playing put him in the spotlight in King Oliver's band. By the end of their national tour, Louie Armstrong was a famous man.

In 1924, Armstrong moved to Harlem to join Fletcher Henderson's world famous band. While in the band, Louis started playing the trumpet, the instrument that he is most famous for. Armstrong starred in the musical *Hot Chocolates,* which brought him even more fame. Later, he played for England's King George on a tour of Europe.

Armstrong's rough singing voice earned him the nickname "Satchelmouth" or "Satchmo." Before he died in 1971, Louie "Satchmo" Armstrong toured the world several times and made over fifty movies. From a life of poverty in New Orleans to the world famous "King of Swing," Louis Armstrong showed the world what a jazzman can do.

Edward Kennedy "Duke" Ellington — 1899-1974
Bandleader

Another shining star in Harlem's swinging jazz age was Duke Ellington. In his lifetime, Duke composed over 6,000 songs. He wrote scores for five movies and several musicals. His famous works have been played and recorded by thousands of musicians. And all this music was produced by someone who had to be forced to practice piano as a child.

Edward Kennedy Ellington was born in Washington, D.C. His friends nicknamed him "Duke" because he was always "duked out" in the finest clothes. Baseball and art were Duke's favorite hobbies while growing up. He disliked practicing piano while his friends were outside playing ball. When he finished high school, Ellington was offered a scholarship to Pratt Institute of Art in New York City. By then, Duke wanted a career in music.

Duke worked at a soda fountain called the Poodle Dog Cafe. The cafe had a band, and sometimes Ellington was asked to sit in. Inspired by the cafe, Duke wrote his first song, "The Soda Fountain Rag." Before long, Ellington was playing professionally.

58

Ellington took his band to New York City in 1922 where he met blues great Fats Waller and other influential musicians. One year later, Ellington's band became a regular at the Hollywood Club at Forty-ninth and Broadway. In 1927, Ellington began playing at Harlem's world famous Cotton Club.

The Cotton Club was the location of a weekly radio broadcast that was heard in cities all over the country. Soon, Ellington's theme song, "East St. Louis Toodle-Oo," was broadcast nationwide. Ellington continued to play the Cotton Club for the next five years.

The thirties were the time of the Depression. People could not afford to go to nightclubs and Ellington's brand of swing music lost some of its popularity. Ellington, however, continued to compose. He kept his band together while losing money on them. He said, "A musical profit is more important than a financial loss."

Ellington's fame continued to spread after World War II, and he continued to play throughout the world. By the time he died in 1974, Duke Ellington had become a legend in his own time. He had brought the joy of swing to the lives of millions of people.

During the twenties, the Cotton Club was one of the most popular night clubs in Harlem.

A FINAL WORD

The early 1900's were an incredible time of growth for the black race. Freed of the bonds of slavery, black people educated themselves. They became scientists, inventors, musicians, politicians, actors, artists, and more. Although prejudice continued to hold them back, tens-of-thousands of black men and women rose above its evil grip and changed the world for the better. Unfortunately, space does not allow room for all of their stories.

The Harlem Renaissance of the twenties was one of the brightest spots for black people during the twentieth century. When the Depression hit in 1930, businesses closed down and 14 million people were thrown out of work across the country. Black people were the first to be fired when the hard times hit. Black schools were the first to have their funds cut. Black artists suffered. Nightclubs shut down and theaters closed their doors. A mood of despair fell across the cities of America. The hard times of most black people got even harder.

But the outstanding works of greats like Duke Ellington, Langston Hughes, and others continued to give hope to people caught in a web of poverty and prejudice. Their words, arts, and music shine today like they did in the twenties. Society will remember their contributions for years to come.

INDEX